THE BEST OF NIRVANA

ISBN 978-0-7935-8960-9

HAL•LEONARD®
CORPORATION
7777 W. BLUEMOUND RD. P.O. BOX 13819 MILWAUKEE, WI 53213

Visit Hal Leonard Online at
www.halleonard.com

STRUM AND PICK PATTERNS

This chart contains the suggested strum and pick patterns that are referred to by number at the beginning of each song in this book. The symbols ⊓ and ∨ in the strum patterns refer to down and up strokes, respectively. The letters in the pick patterns indicate which right-hand fingers plays which strings.

p = **thumb**
i = **index finger**
m = **middle finger**
a = **ring finger**

For example; Pick Pattern 2
is played: thumb - index - middle - ring

Strum Patterns   ## Pick Patterns

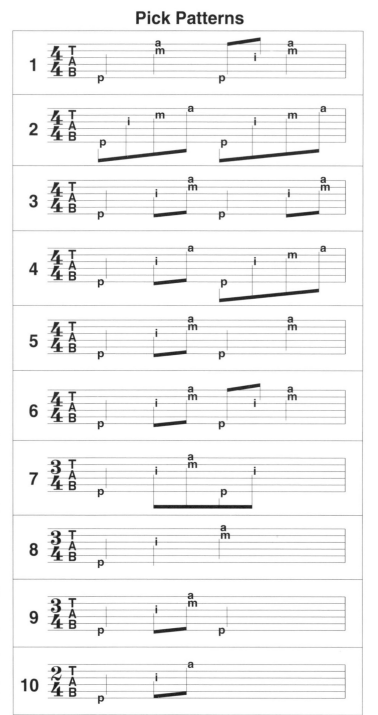

You can use the 3/4 Strum or Pick Patterns in songs written in compound meter (6/8, 9/8, 12/8, etc.).
For example, you can accompany a song in 6/8 by playing the 3/4 pattern twice in each measure.
The 4/4 Strum and Pick Patterns can be used for songs written in cut time (¢) by doubling the note time values in the patterns. Each pattern would therefore last two measures in cut time.

About a Girl

Words and Music by Kurt Cobain

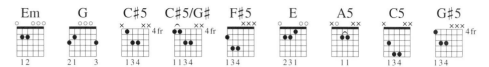

Strum Pattern: 2
Pick Pattern: 4

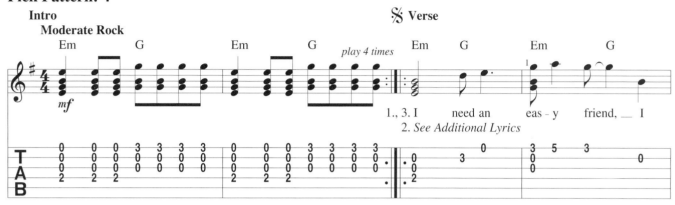

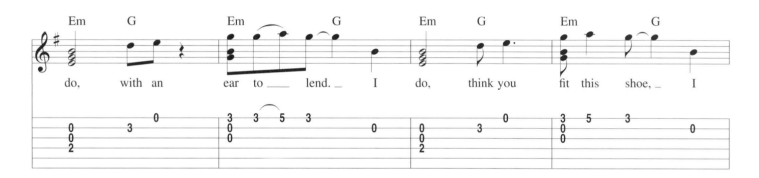

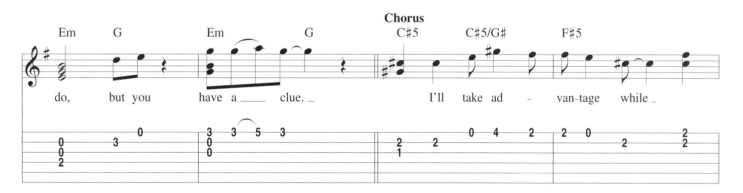

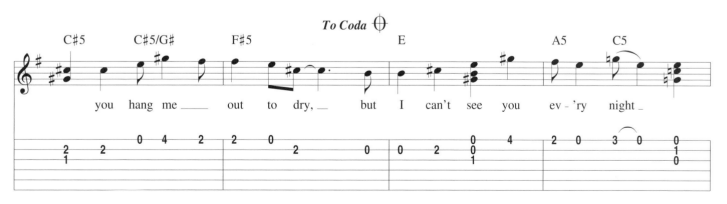

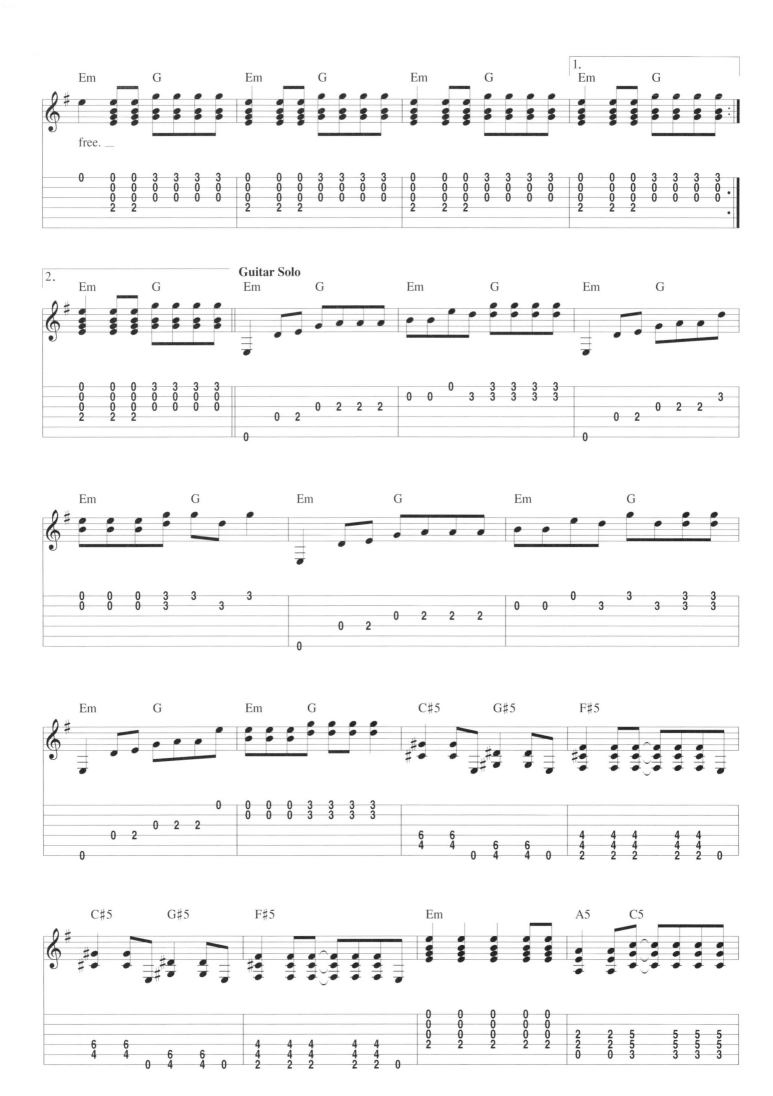

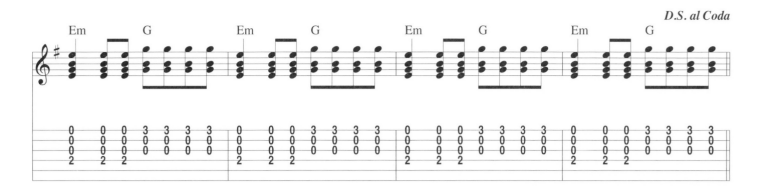

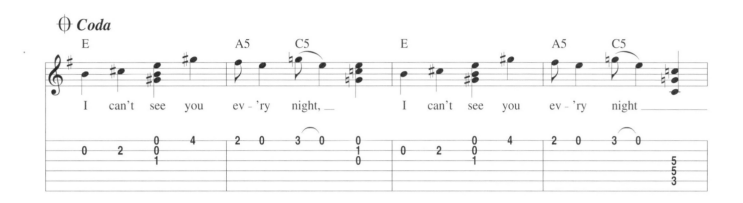

*Use Pattern 10

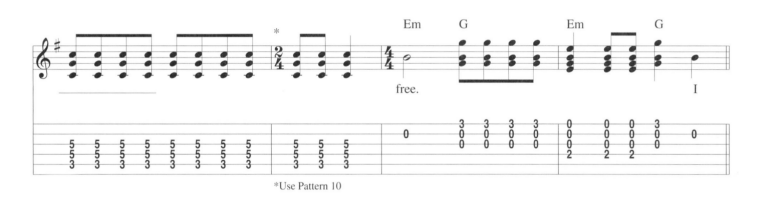

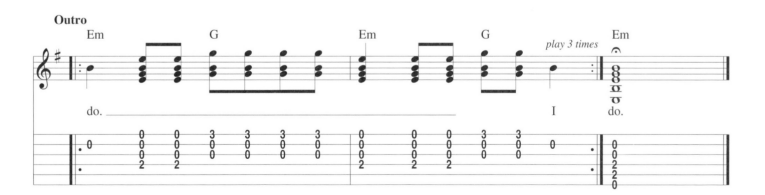

Additional Lyrics

2. I'm standing in your line,
    I do, hope you have the time.
    I do, pick a number to,
    I do, keep a date with you.

All Apologies

Words and Music by Kurt Cobain

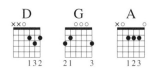

Strum Pattern: 3, 4
Pick Pattern: 1, 2

Intro
Moderately

Verse

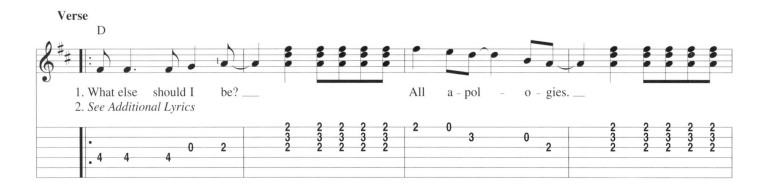

1. What else should I be? ___ All a‑pol‑o‑gies. ___
2. *See Additional Lyrics*

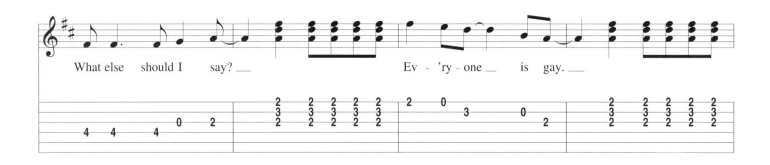

What else should I say? ___ Ev‑'ry‑one ___ is gay. ___

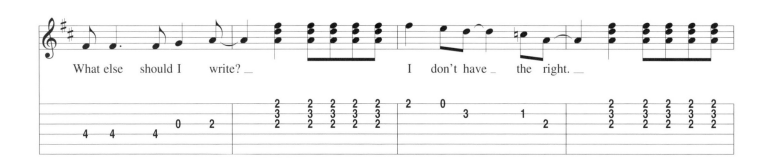

What else should I write? ___ I don't have ___ the right. ___

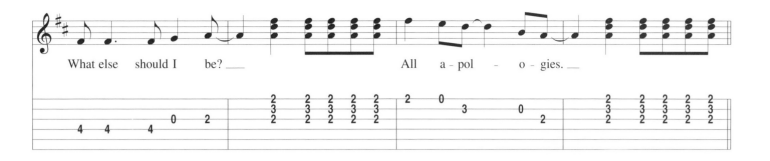

What else should I be? ___ All a - pol - o - gies. ___

Chorus

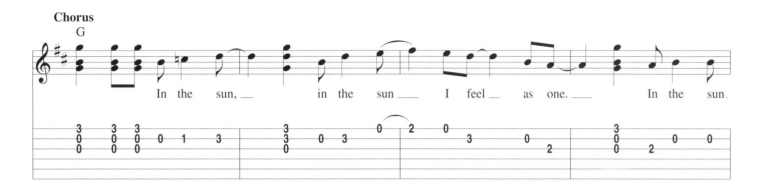

In the sun, ___ in the sun ___ I feel ___ as one. In the sun.

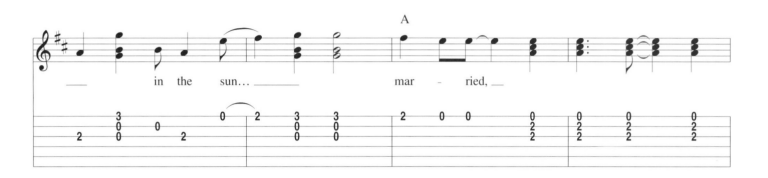

___ in the sun... ___ mar - ried, ___

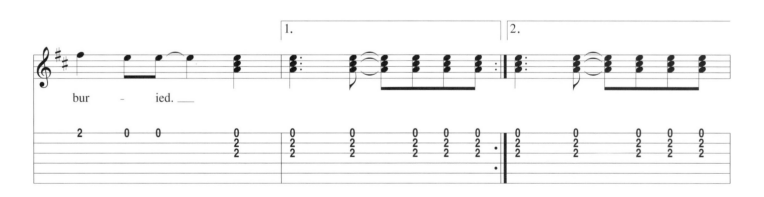

bur - ied. ___

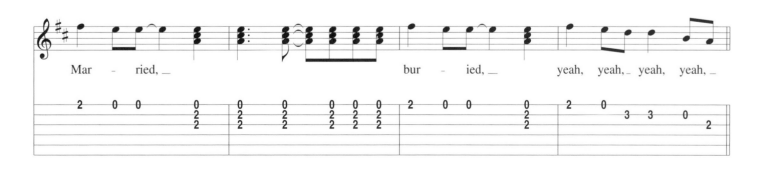

Mar - ried, ___ bur - ied, ___ yeah, yeah, ___ yeah, yeah, ___

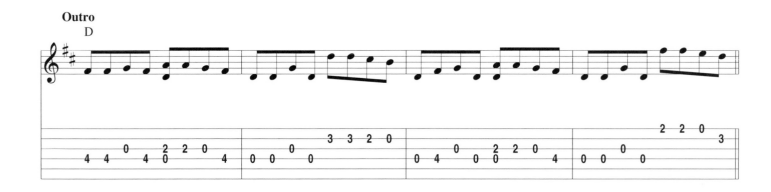

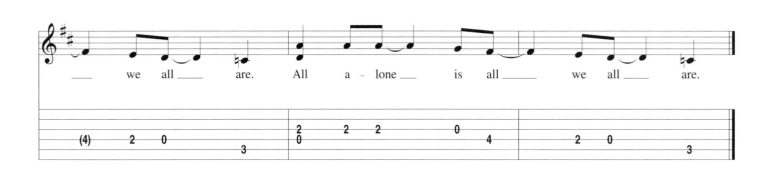

Additional Lyrics

2. I wish I was like you, easily amused.
Find my nest of salt. Ev'rything is my fault.
I'll take all the blame, aqua seafoam shame.
Sunburn, freezer burn. Choking on the ashes of her enemy.

Come as You Are

Words and Music by Kurt Cobain

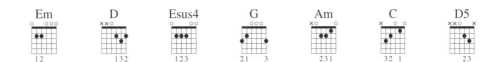

 Strum Pattern: 3
Pick Pattern: 3

Intro
Heavy Rock

play 3 times

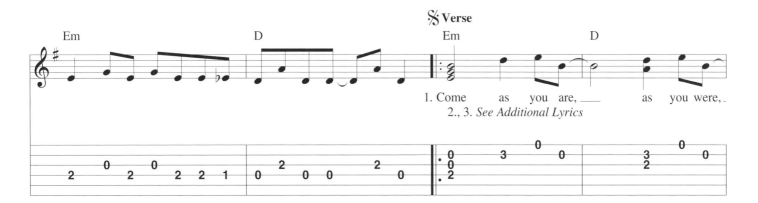

§ **Verse**

1. Come as you are, ___ as you were, ___
2., 3. *See Additional Lyrics*

___ as I want you to be, ___ as a friend, ___ as a friend, ___

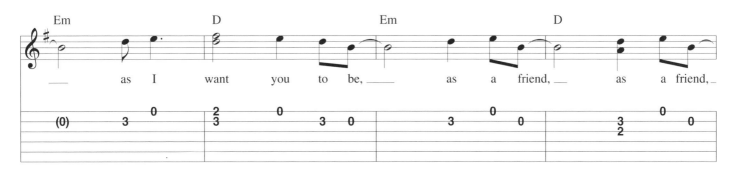

1. ___ as an old en-e-my.

2., 3. old mem-o-ry. ___

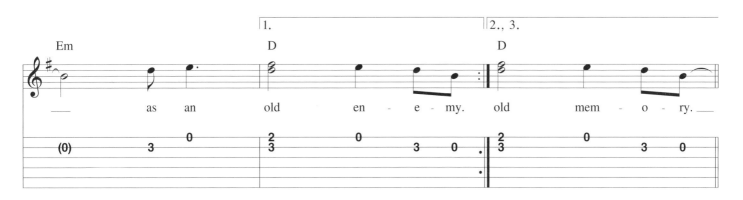

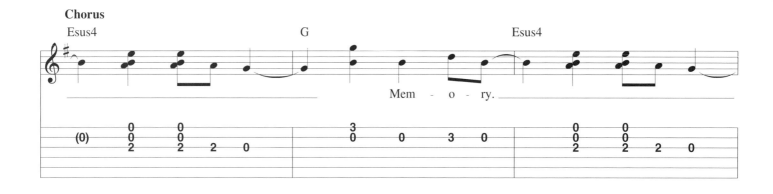

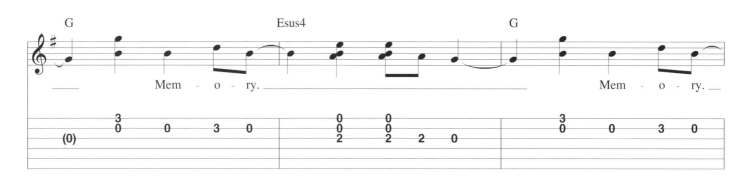

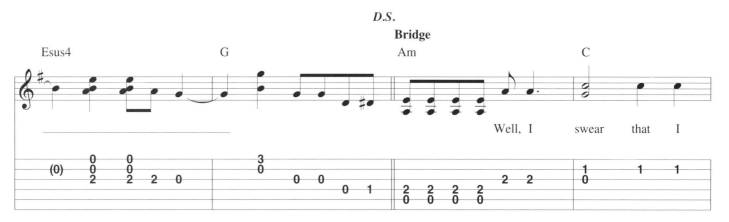

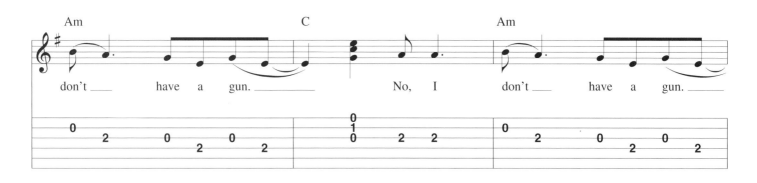

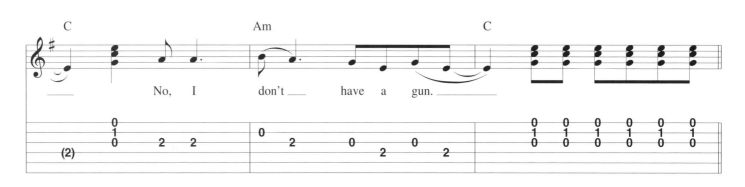

Interlude

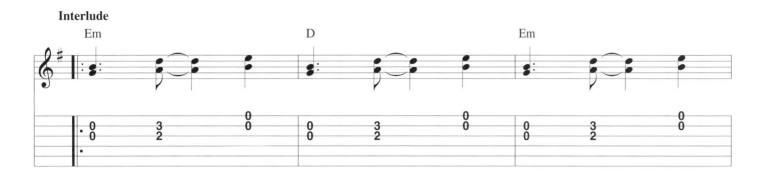

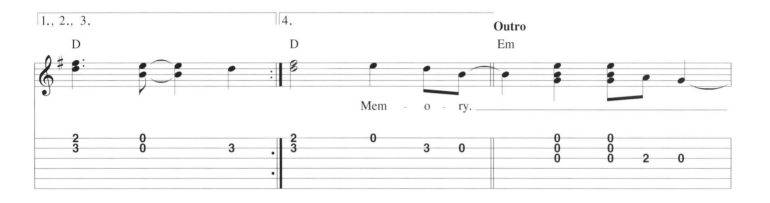

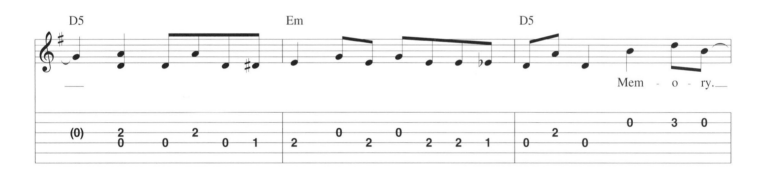

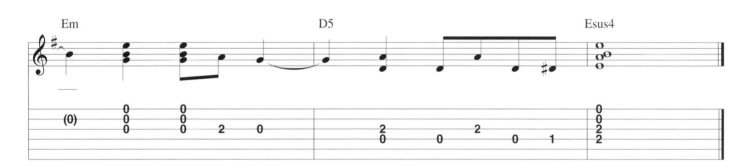

Additional Lyrics

2. Take your time, hurry up,
   The choice is yours, don't be late.
   Take a rest, as a friend,
   As an old memory.

3. Come doused in mud, served in bleach,
   As I want you to be.
   As a trend, as a friend,
   As an old memory.

Blew

Words and Music by Kurt Cobain

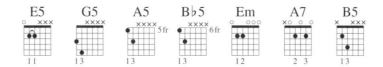

Strum Pattern: 2, 4
Pick Pattern: 1, 3

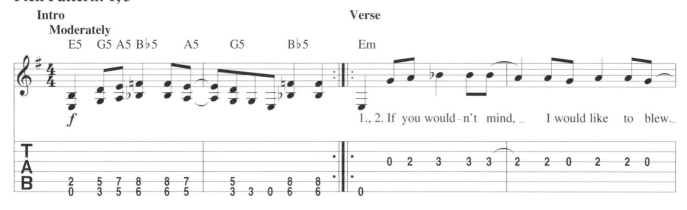

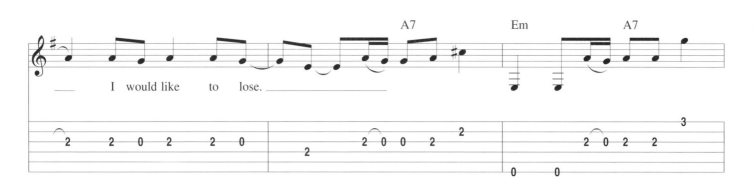

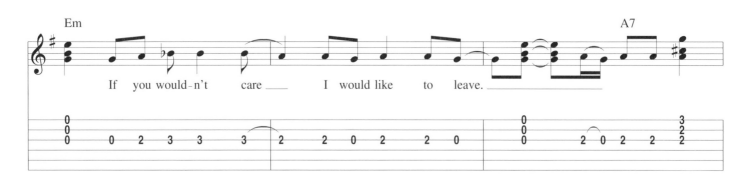

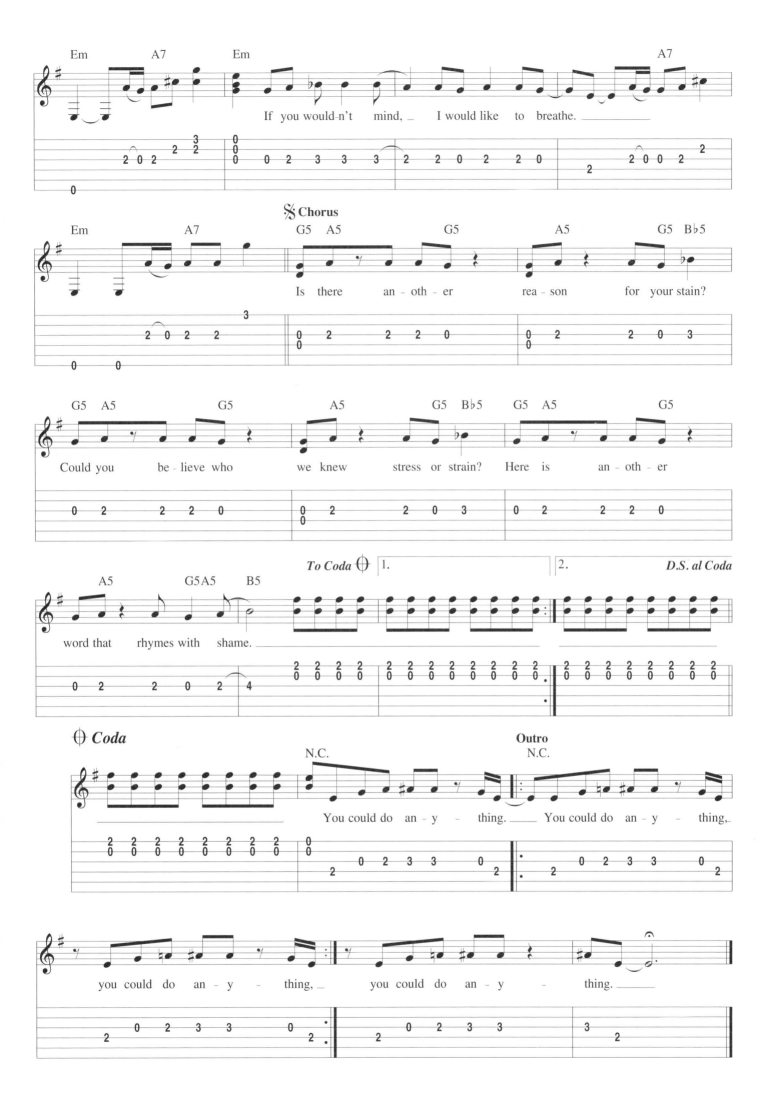

Breed

Words and Music by Kurt Cobain

Strum Pattern: 1, 3
Pick Pattern: 2, 4

Additional Lyrics

2., 4. Get away, get away, get away,
Get away, way, way from your home.
I'm afraid, I'm afraid, I'm afraid,
I'm afraid, of a ghost.

Heart Shaped Box

Words and Music by Kurt Cobain

Strum Pattern: 1, 3
Pick Pattern: 2, 4

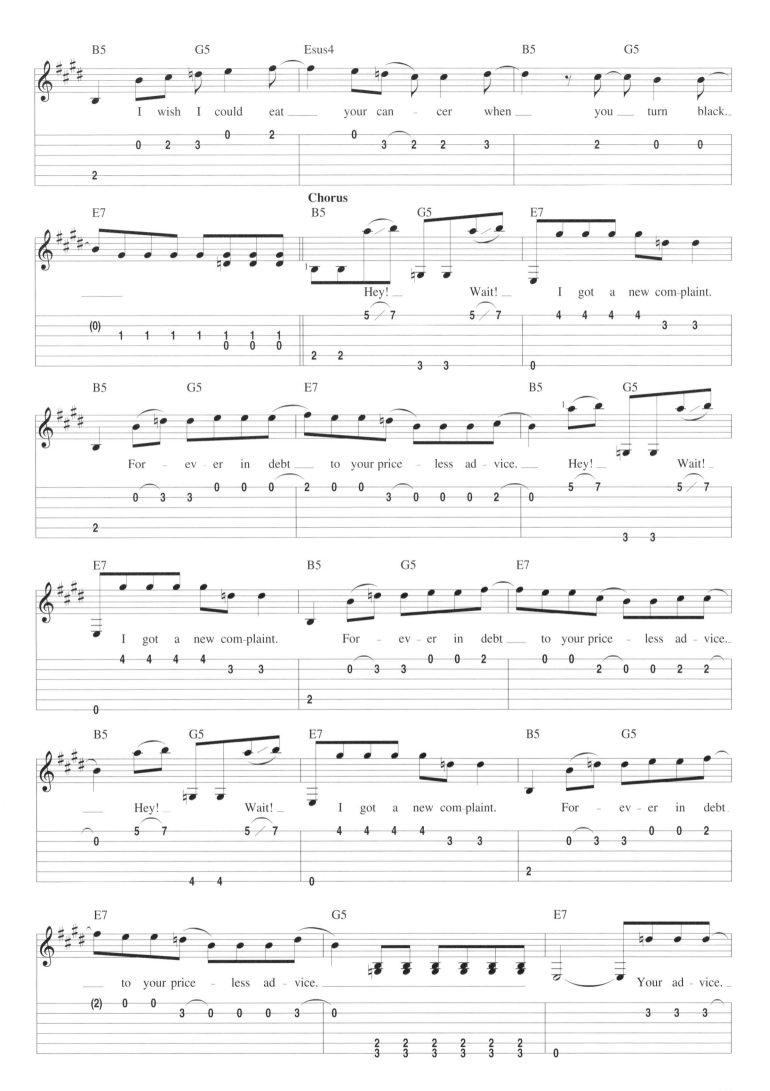

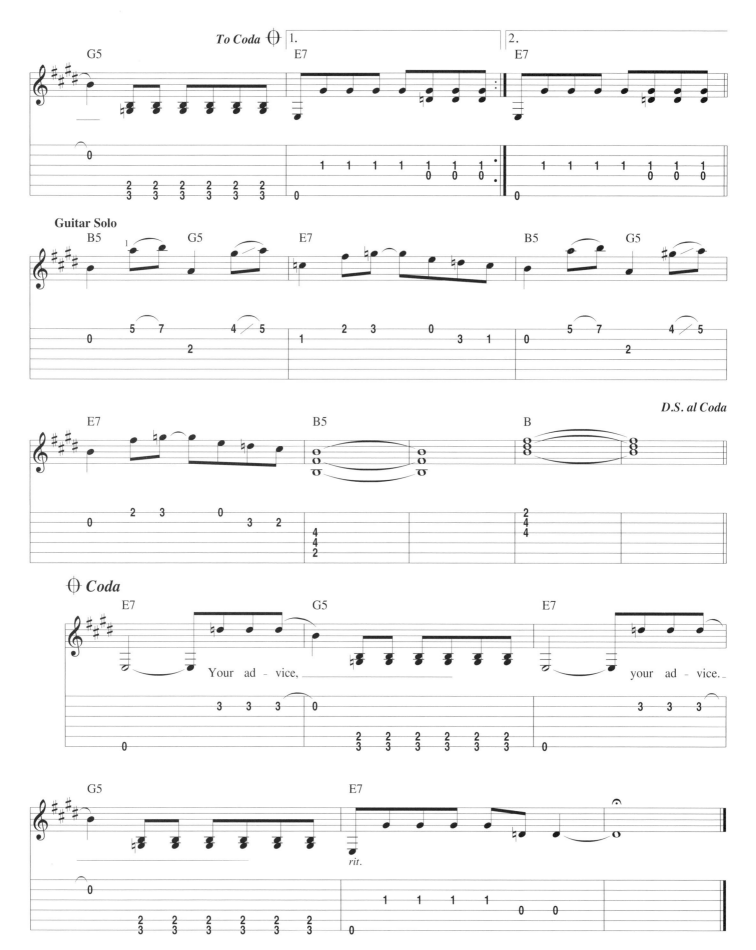

Additional Lyrics

2. Meat eating orchids forgive no one just yet.
   Cut myself on angel hair and baby's breath.
   Broken hymen of your highness, I'm left black.
   Throw down your umbilical noose so I can climb right back.

In Bloom

Words and Music by Kurt Cobain

Strum Pattern: 1, 3
Pick Pattern: 2, 4

Intro
Moderately Slow

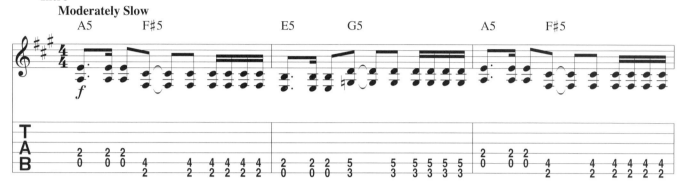

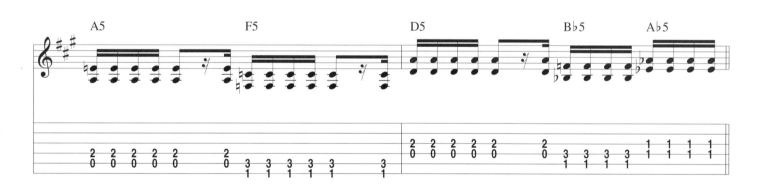

Verse

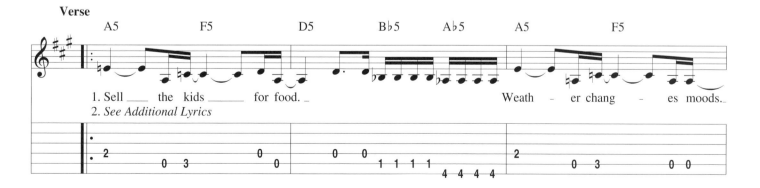

1. Sell ___ the kids ___ for food. ___   Weath – er chang – es moods. ___
2. *See Additional Lyrics*

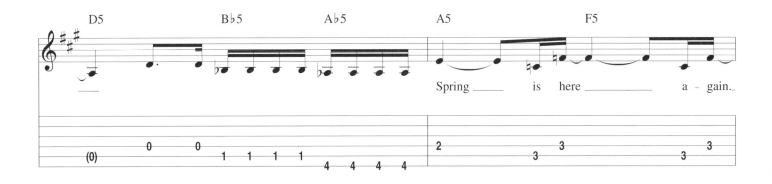

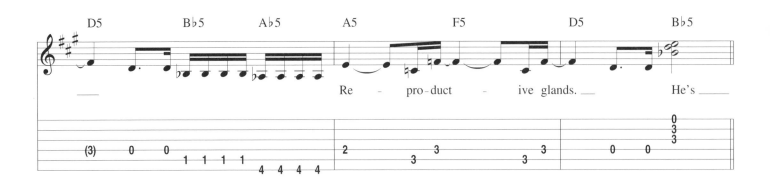

𝄋 Chorus

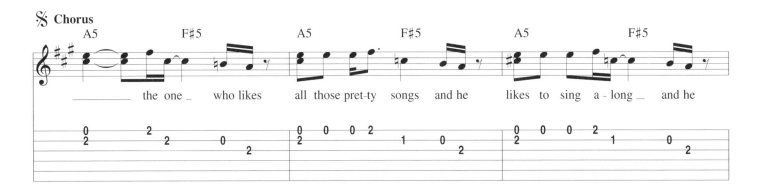

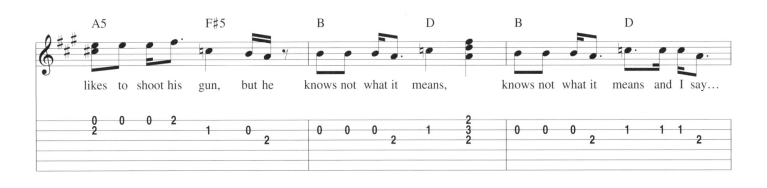

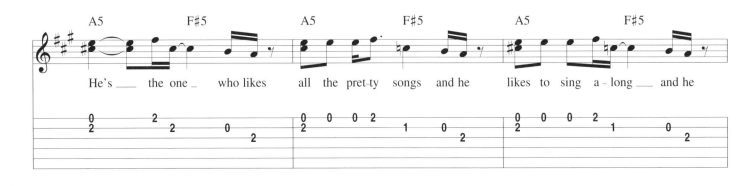

Additional Lyrics

2. We can have some more.
   Nature is a whore.
   Bruises on the fruit.
   Tender age in bloom.

The Man Who Sold the World

Words and Music by David Bowie

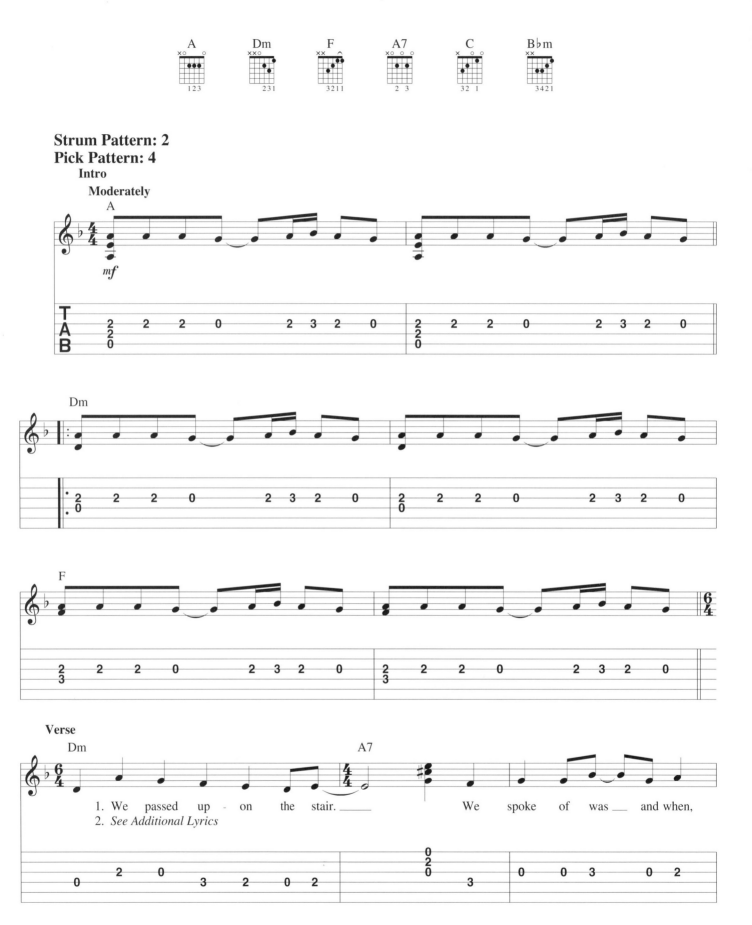

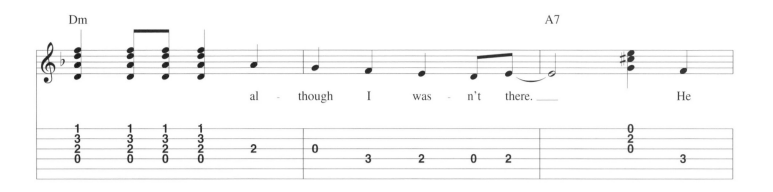

al - though I was - n't there. _____ He

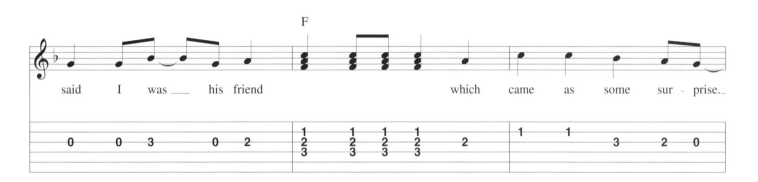

said I was _____ his friend which came as some sur - prise. _____

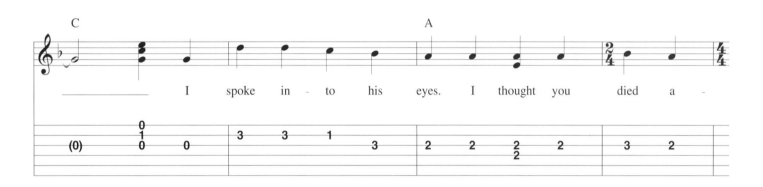

_____ I spoke in - to his eyes. I thought you died a -

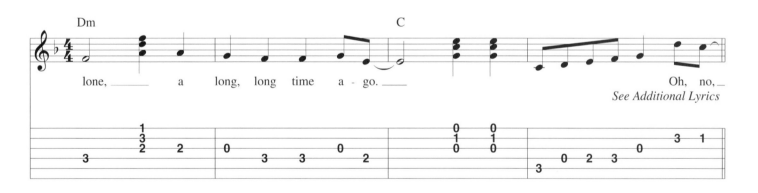

lone, _____ a long, long time a - go. _____ Oh, no, _____

See Additional Lyrics

% **Chorus**

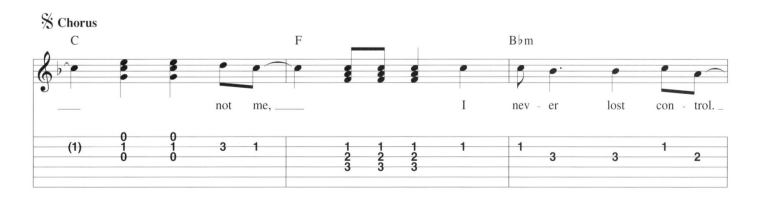

not me, _____ I nev - er lost con - trol. _____

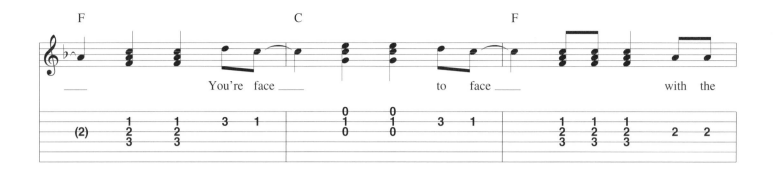

You're face _____ to face _____ with the

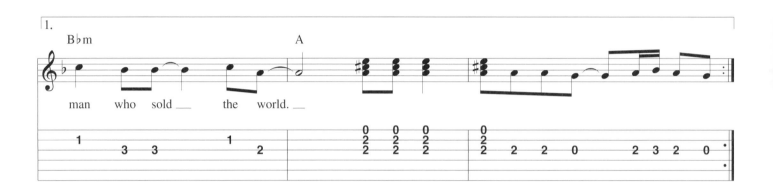

1.

man who sold ___ the world. _____

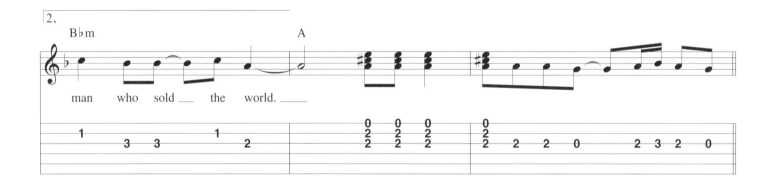

2.

man who sold ___ the world. _____

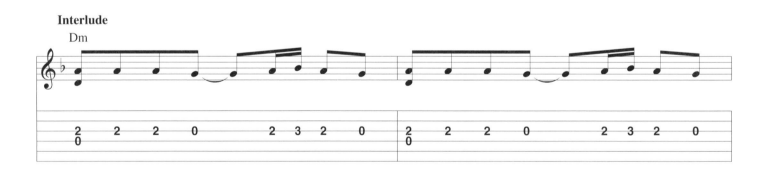

Interlude

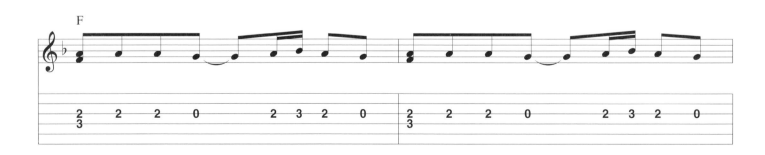

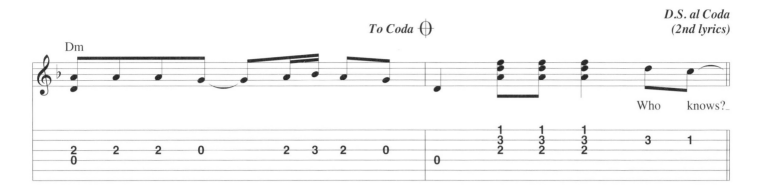

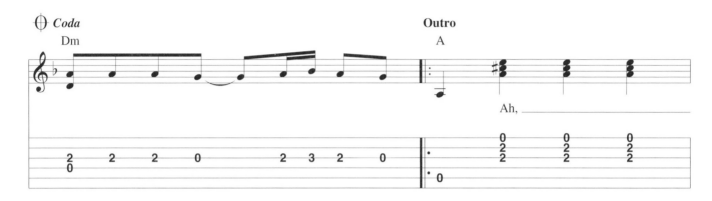

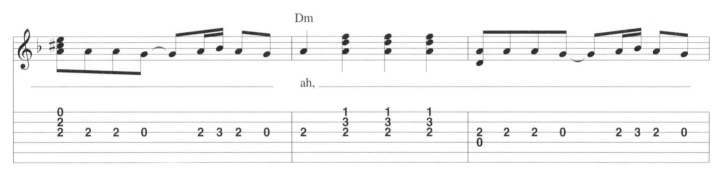

Repeat and Fade

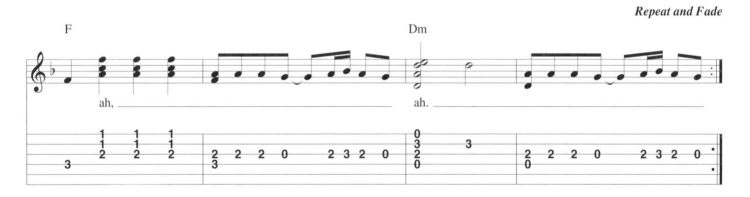

Additional Lyrics

2. I laughed and shook his hand,
   And made my way back home.
   I searched for form and land,
   For years and years I roamed.
   I gazed a gazely stare
   At all the millions here.
   We must have died alone,
   A long, long time ago.

Chorus   Who knows? Not me,
   We never lost control.
   You're face to face with the
   Man who sold the world.

Lithium

Words and Music by Kurt Cobain

Chorus

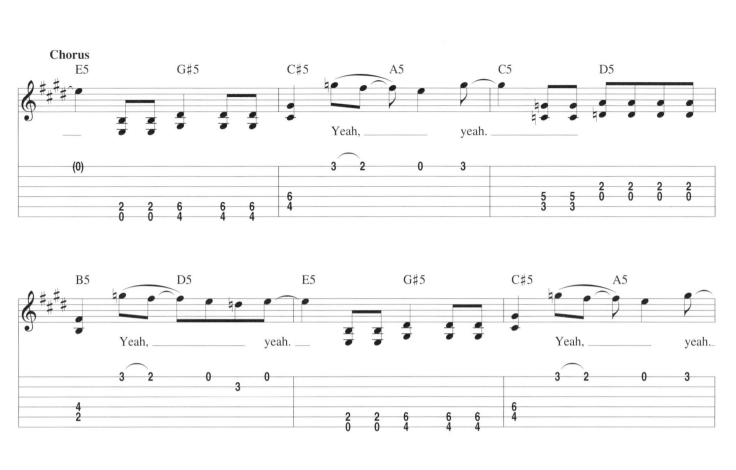

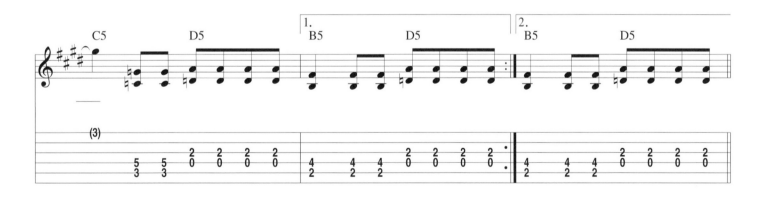

Bridge

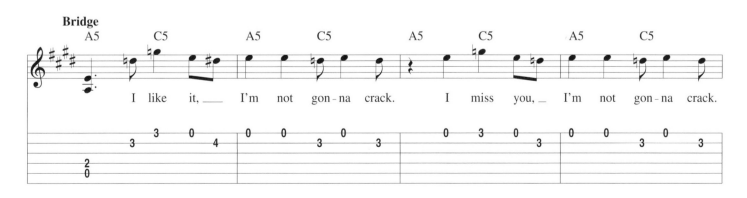

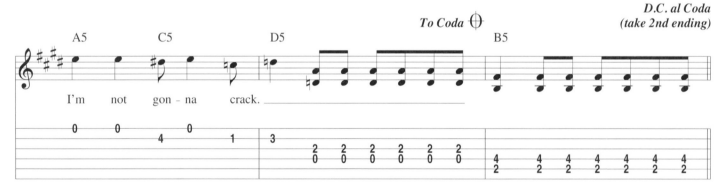

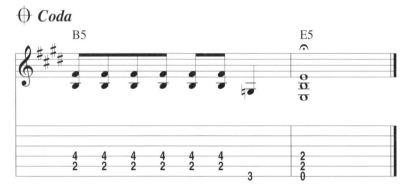

Additional Lyrics

2. I'm so happy 'cause today I shaved my head; I'm not sad.
And just maybe I'm to blame for all I've heard; I'm not sure.
I'm so excited; I can't wait to meet you there, but I don't care.
I'm so horny; that's okay, my will is good.

Mr. Moustache

Words and Music by Kurt Cobain

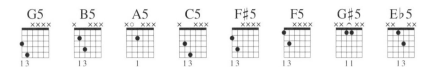

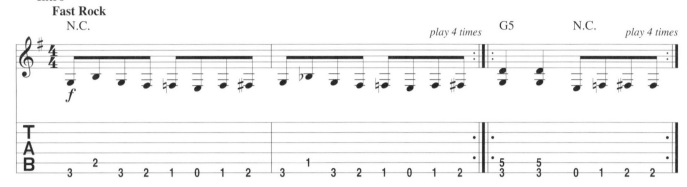

Strum Pattern: 2, 4
Pick Pattern: 1, 3

Intro
Fast Rock

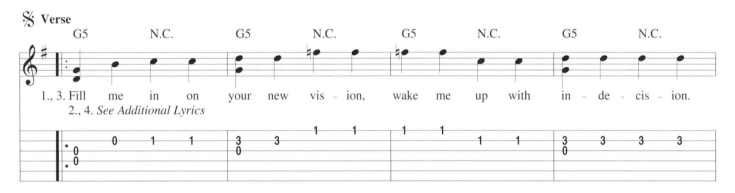

 Verse

1., 3. Fill me in on your new vis - ion, wake me up with in - de - cis - ion.
2., 4. *See Additional Lyrics*

Help me trust your might - y wis - dom, yes, I eat cow, I am not proud. _

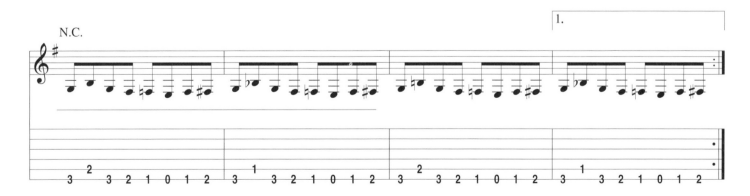

Additional Lyrics

2., 4. Show me how you question question,
Lead the way to my temptation.
Take my hand and give it cleaning,
Yes, I eat cow, I am not proud.

On a Plain

Words and Music by Kurt Cobain

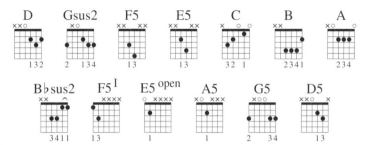

Strum Pattern: 1, 3
Pick Pattern: 2, 4

Intro
Moderately

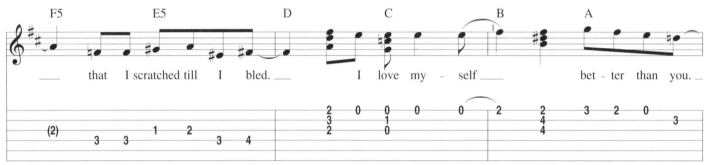

1. I'll start this off _____ with-out an-y words. _____ I got so high _____
2., 3. *See Additional Lyrics*

_____ that I scratched till I bled. _____ I love my-self _____ bet-ter than you. _____

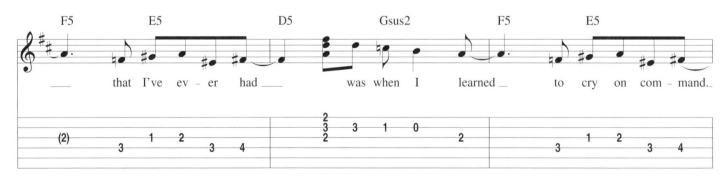

_____ I know it's wrong. _____ So, what should I do? _____ The fin-est day _____

_____ that I've ev-er had _____ was when I learned _____ to cry on com-mand. _____

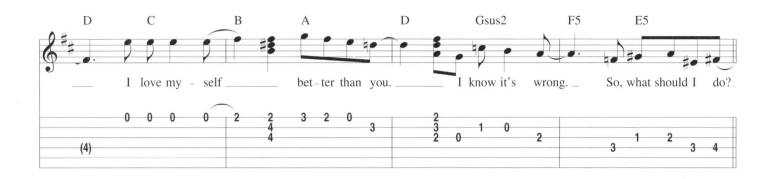

I love my - self _____ bet - ter than you. _____ I know it's wrong. ___ So, what should I do?

Chorus

I'm on a plain. ___

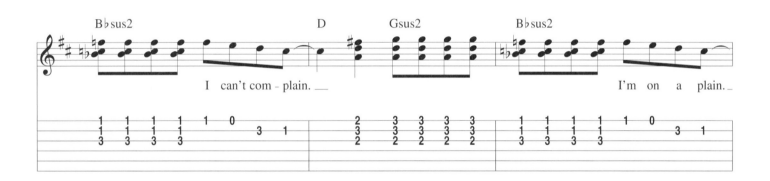

I can't com - plain. ___   I'm on a plain. ___

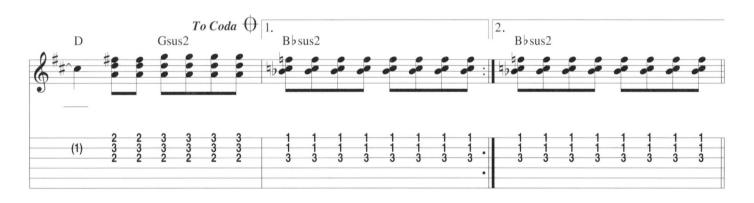

To Coda ⊕ | 1. | 2.

Bridge

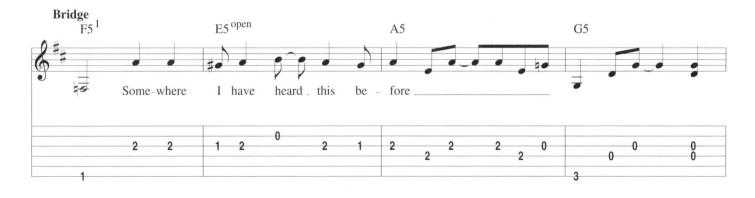

Some-where I have heard this be - fore _____

Additional Lyrics

2. My brother died every night.
   It's safe to say, don't quote me on that.
   I love myself better than you.
   I know it's wrong. So, what should I do?
   The black sheep got blackmailed again.
   Forgot to put on the zip code.
   I love myself better than you.
   I know it's wrong. So, what should I do?

3. It is now time to make it unclear,
   To write off lines that don't make sense.
   I love myself better than you.
   I know it's wrong. So, what should I do?
   And one more special message to go,
   And then I'm done, then I can go home.
   I love myself better than you.
   I know it's wrong. So, what should I do?

Penny Royal Tea

Words and Music by Kurt Cobain

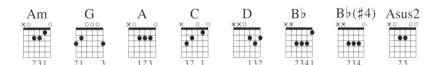

Strum Pattern: 3
Pick Pattern: 2, 4

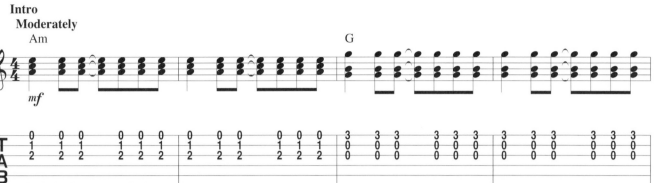

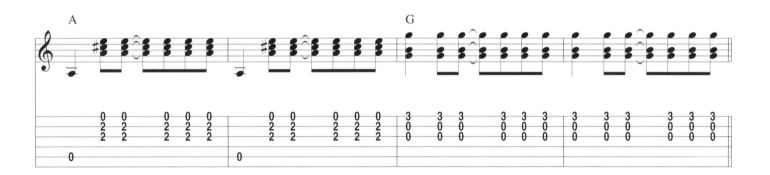

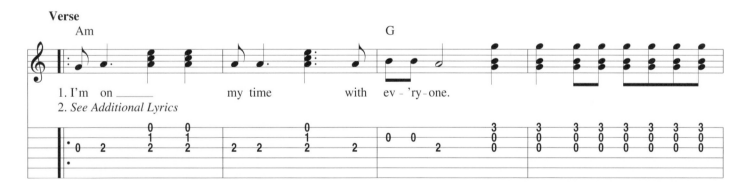

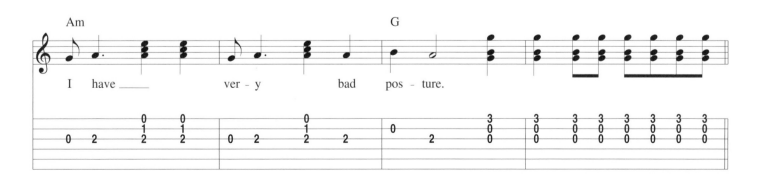

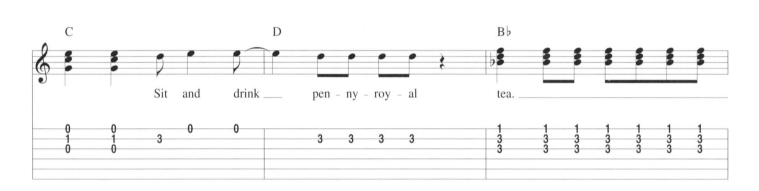

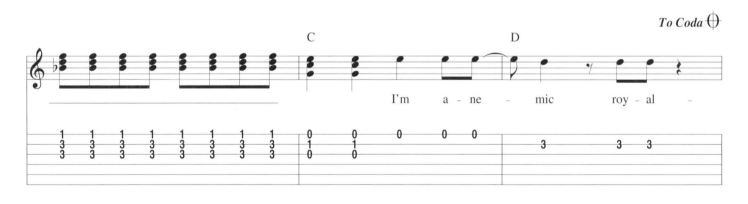

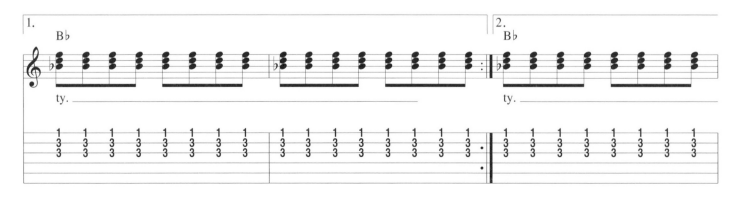

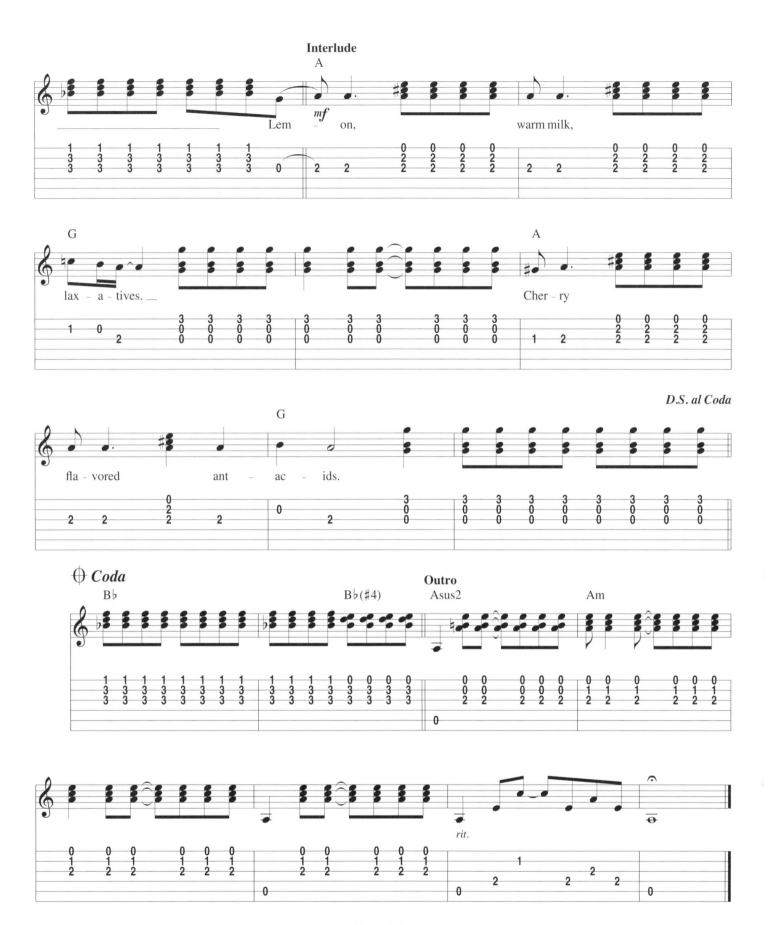

Additional Lyrics

2. Give me landing for afterward
    So I can't stay termin'ly.

Chorus I'm so tired I can't sleep
          I'm anemic royalty.
          I'm a liar and a thief.
          I'm anemic royalty.

Rape Me

Words and Music by Kurt Cobain

Additional Lyrics

2. Hate me.
   Do it and do it again.
   Waste me.
   Taste me, my friend.

(New Wave) Polly

Words and Music by Kurt Cobain

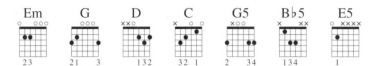

Strum Pattern: 1, 6
Pick Pattern: 3, 4

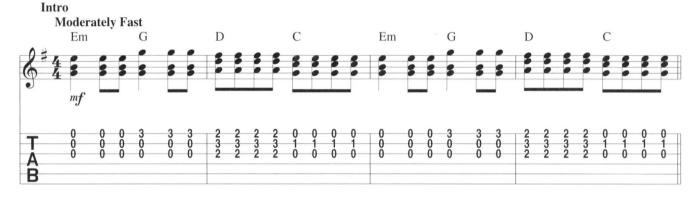

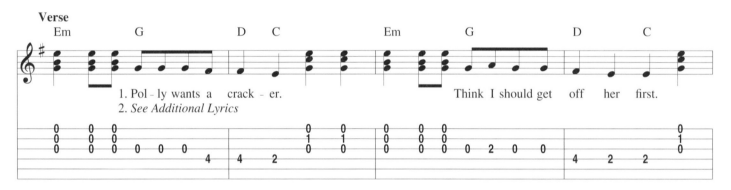

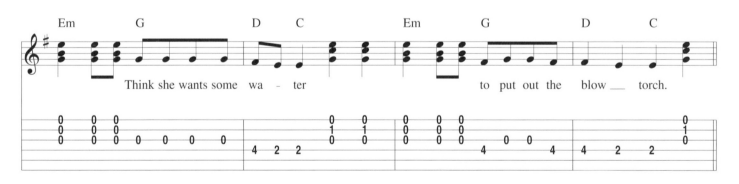

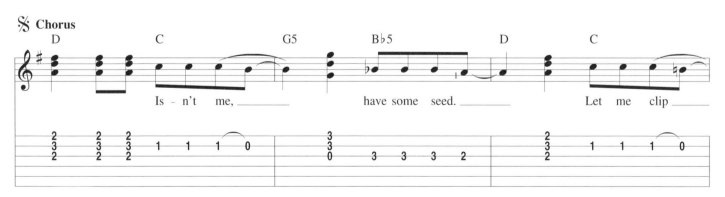

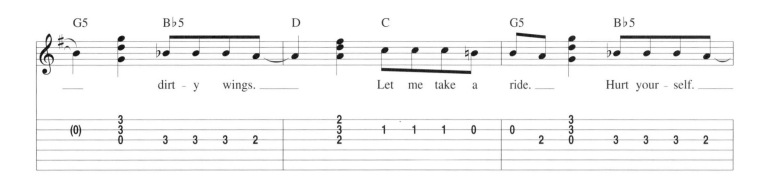

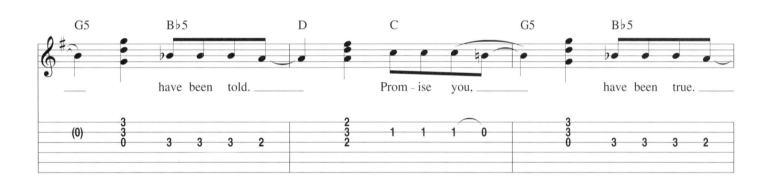

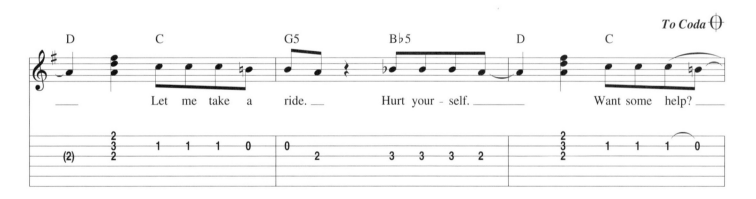

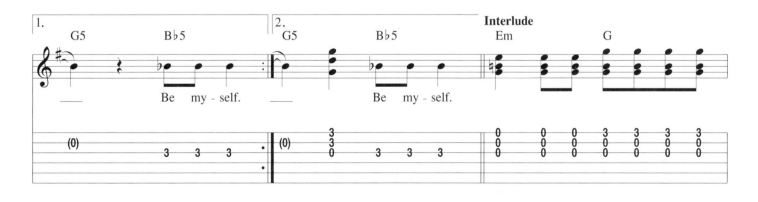

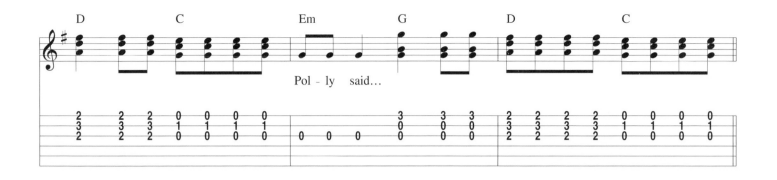

Pol - ly said...

Verse

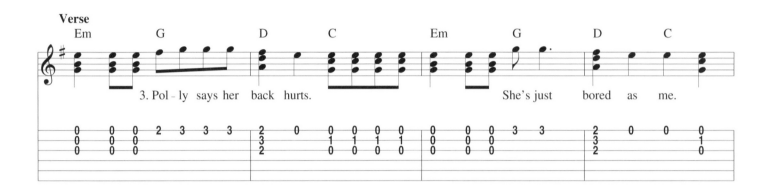

3. Pol - ly says her back hurts. She's just bored as me.

D.S. al Coda

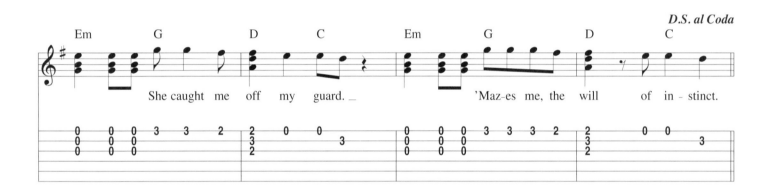

She caught me off my guard. ___ 'Maz-es me, the will of in - stinct.

⊕ Coda

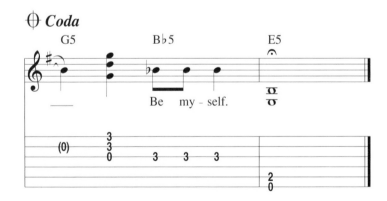

G5   Bb5   E5

___   Be my - self.

Additional Lyrics

2. Polly wants a cracker.
   Maybe she would like some food.
   She asked me to untie her.
   Chase would be nice for a few.

Smells Like Teen Spirit

Words and Music by Kurt Cobain, Chris Novoselic and David Grohl

Strum Pattern: 1, 3
Pick Pattern: 2, 4

Additional Lyrics

2. I'm worse at what I do best,
And for this gift I feel blessed.
Our little group has always been
And always will until the end.

3. And I forget just why I taste.
Oh yeah, I guess it makes me smile.
I found it hard, it was hard to find.
Oh, well, whatever, nevermind.

Stain

Words and Music by Kurt Cobain

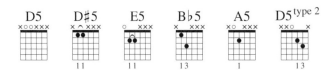

Strum Pattern: 1
Pick Pattern: 3

Intro
Fast Rock

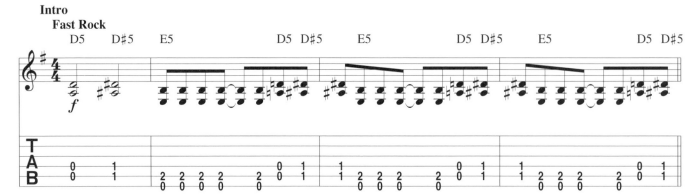

Verse

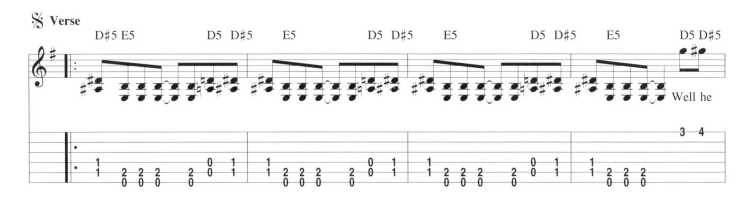

Well he

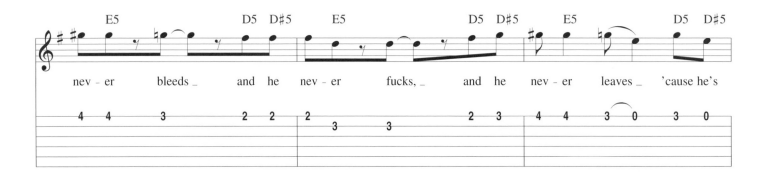

nev-er bleeds _ and he nev-er fucks, _ and he nev-er leaves _ 'cause he's

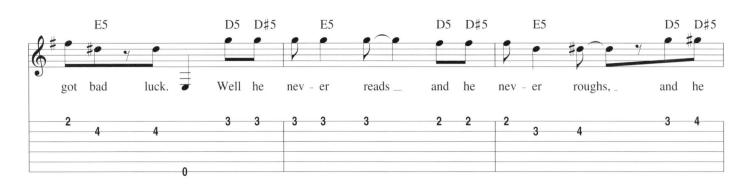

got bad luck. Well he nev-er reads _ and he nev-er roughs, _ and he

EASY GUITAR
WITH NOTES & TAB

This series features simplified arrangements with notes, tab, chord charts, and strum and pick patterns.

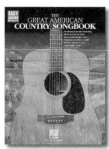

MIXED FOLIOS

00702287	Acoustic	$19.99
00702002	Acoustic Rock Hits for Easy Guitar	$17.99
00702166	All-Time Best Guitar Collection	$29.99
00702232	Best Acoustic Songs for Easy Guitar	$16.99
00119835	Best Children's Songs	$16.99
00703055	The Big Book of Nursery Rhymes & Children's Songs	$16.99
00698978	Big Christmas Collection	$19.99
00702394	Bluegrass Songs for Easy Guitar	$15.99
00289632	Bohemian Rhapsody	$19.99
00703387	Celtic Classics	$16.99
00224808	Chart Hits of 2016-2017	$14.99
00267383	Chart Hits of 2017-2018	$14.99
00334293	Chart Hits of 2019-2020	$16.99
00403479	Chart Hits of 2021-2022	$16.99
00702149	Children's Christian Songbook	$9.99
00702028	Christmas Classics	$9.99
00101779	Christmas Guitar	$16.99
00702141	Classic Rock	$8.95
00159642	Classical Melodies	$12.99
00253933	Disney/Pixar's Coco	$19.99
00702203	CMT's 100 Greatest Country Songs	$34.99
00702283	The Contemporary Christian Collection	$16.99
00196954	Contemporary Disney	$19.99
00702239	Country Classics for Easy Guitar	$24.99
00702257	Easy Acoustic Guitar Songs	$17.99
00702041	Favorite Hymns for Easy Guitar	$12.99
00222701	Folk Pop Songs	$19.99
00126894	Frozen	$14.99
00333922	Frozen 2	$14.99
00702286	Glee	$16.99
00702160	The Great American Country Songbook	$19.99
00702148	Great American Gospel for Guitar	$14.99
00702050	Great Classical Themes for Easy Guitar	$9.99
00148030	Halloween Guitar Songs	$17.99
00702273	Irish Songs	$14.99
00192503	Jazz Classics for Easy Guitar	$16.99
00702275	Jazz Favorites for Easy Guitar	$17.99
00702274	Jazz Standards for Easy Guitar	$19.99
00702162	Jumbo Easy Guitar Songbook	$24.99
00232285	La La Land	$16.99
00702258	Legends of Rock	$14.99
00702189	MTV's 100 Greatest Pop Songs	$34.99
00702272	1950s Rock	$16.99
00702271	1960s Rock	$16.99
00702270	1970s Rock	$24.99
00702269	1980s Rock	$16.99
00702268	1990s Rock	$24.99
00369043	Rock Songs for Kids	$14.99
00109725	Once	$14.99
00702187	Selections from O Brother Where Art Thou?	$19.99
00702178	100 Songs for Kids	$16.99
00702515	Pirates of the Caribbean	$17.99
00702125	Praise and Worship for Guitar	$14.99
00287930	Songs from *A Star Is Born, The Greatest Showman, La La Land*, and More Movie Musicals	$16.99
00702285	Southern Rock Hits	$12.99
00156420	Star Wars Music	$16.99
00121535	30 Easy Celtic Guitar Solos	$16.99
00244654	Top Hits of 2017	$14.99
00283786	Top Hits of 2018	$14.99
00302269	Top Hits of 2019	$14.99
00355779	Top Hits of 2020	$14.99
00374083	Top Hits of 2021	$16.99
00702294	Top Worship Hits	$17.99
00702255	VH1's 100 Greatest Hard Rock Songs	$39.99
00702175	VH1's 100 Greatest Songs of Rock and Roll	$34.99
00702253	Wicked	$12.99

ARTIST COLLECTIONS

00702267	AC/DC for Easy Guitar	$17.99
00156221	Adele – 25	$16.99
00396889	Adele – 30	$19.99
00702040	Best of the Allman Brothers	$16.99
00702865	J.S. Bach for Easy Guitar	$15.99
00702169	Best of The Beach Boys	$16.99
00702292	The Beatles — 1	$22.99
00125796	Best of Chuck Berry	$16.99
00702201	The Essential Black Sabbath	$15.99
00702250	blink-182 — Greatest Hits	$19.99
02501615	Zac Brown Band — The Foundation	$19.99
02501621	Zac Brown Band — You Get What You Give	$16.99
00702043	Best of Johnny Cash	$19.99
00702090	Eric Clapton's Best	$16.99
00702086	Eric Clapton — from the Album Unplugged	$17.99
00702202	The Essential Eric Clapton	$19.99
00702053	Best of Patsy Cline	$17.99
00222697	Very Best of Coldplay – 2nd Edition	$17.99
00702229	The Very Best of Creedence Clearwater Revival	$16.99
00702145	Best of Jim Croce	$16.99
00702278	Crosby, Stills & Nash	$12.99
14042809	Bob Dylan	$15.99
00702276	Fleetwood Mac — Easy Guitar Collection	$17.99
00139462	The Very Best of Grateful Dead	$17.99
00702136	Best of Merle Haggard	$19.99
00702227	Jimi Hendrix — Smash Hits	$19.99
00702288	Best of Hillsong United	$12.99
00702236	Best of Antonio Carlos Jobim	$15.99
00702245	Elton John — Greatest Hits 1970–2002	$19.99
00129855	Jack Johnson	$17.99
00702204	Robert Johnson	$16.99
00702234	Selections from Toby Keith — 35 Biggest Hits	$12.95
00702003	Kiss	$16.99
00702216	Lynyrd Skynyrd	$17.99
00702182	The Essential Bob Marley	$17.99
00146081	Maroon 5	$14.99
00121925	Bruno Mars – Unorthodox Jukebox	$12.99
00702248	Paul McCartney — All the Best	$14.99
00125484	The Best of MercyMe	$12.99
00702209	Steve Miller Band — Young Hearts (Greatest Hits)	$12.95
00124167	Jason Mraz	$15.99
00702096	Best of Nirvana	$17.99
00702211	The Offspring — Greatest Hits	$17.99
00138026	One Direction	$17.99
00702030	Best of Roy Orbison	$17.99
00702144	Best of Ozzy Osbourne	$14.99
00702279	Tom Petty	$17.99
00102911	Pink Floyd	$17.99
00702139	Elvis Country Favorites	$19.99
00702293	The Very Best of Prince	$22.99
00699415	Best of Queen for Guitar	$16.99
00109279	Best of R.E.M.	$14.99
00702208	Red Hot Chili Peppers — Greatest Hits	$19.99
00198960	The Rolling Stones	$17.99
00174793	The Very Best of Santana	$16.99
00702196	Best of Bob Seger	$16.99
00146046	Ed Sheeran	$19.99
00702252	Frank Sinatra — Nothing But the Best	$12.99
00702010	Best of Rod Stewart	$17.99
00702049	Best of George Strait	$17.99
00702259	Taylor Swift for Easy Guitar	$15.99
00359800	Taylor Swift – Easy Guitar Anthology	$24.99
00702260	Taylor Swift — Fearless	$14.99
00139727	Taylor Swift — 1989	$19.99
00115960	Taylor Swift — Red	$16.99
00253667	Taylor Swift — Reputation	$17.99
00702290	Taylor Swift — Speak Now	$16.99
00232849	Chris Tomlin Collection – 2nd Edition	$14.99
00702226	Chris Tomlin — See the Morning	$12.95
00148643	Train	$14.99
00702427	U2 — 18 Singles	$19.99
00702108	Best of Stevie Ray Vaughan	$17.99
00279005	The Who	$14.99
00702123	Best of Hank Williams	$15.99
00194548	Best of John Williams	$14.99
00702228	Neil Young — Greatest Hits	$17.99
00119133	Neil Young — Harvest	$16.99

Prices, contents and availability subject to change without notice.

HAL•LEONARD®

Visit Hal Leonard online at halleonard.com